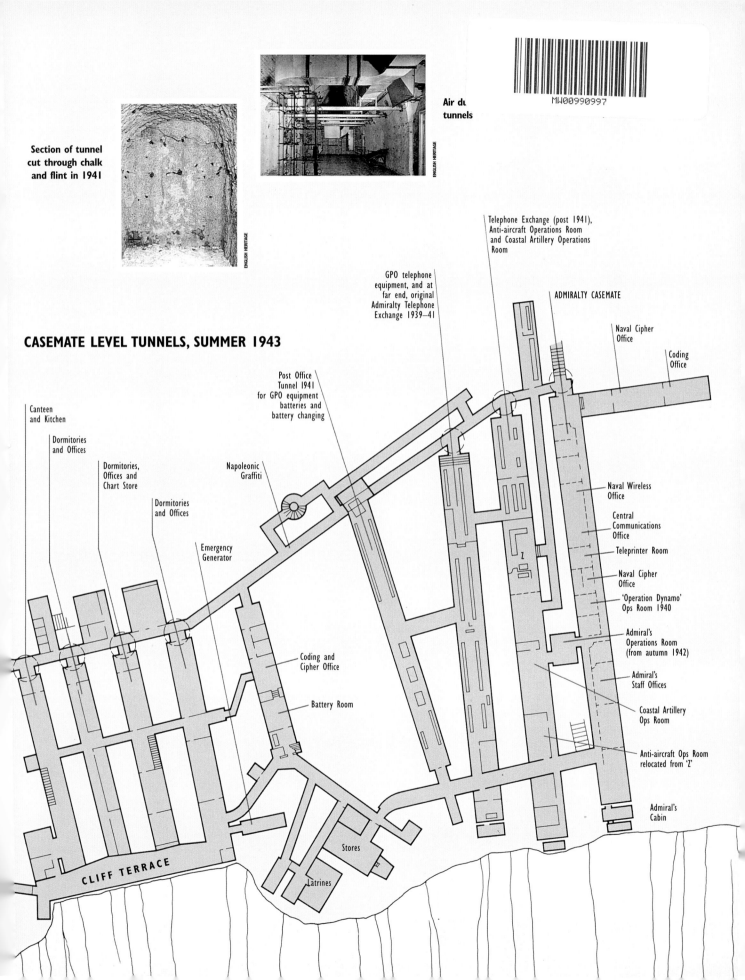

Section of tunnel
cut through chalk
and flint in 1941

ENGLISH HERITAGE

Air du
tunnels

ENGLISH HERITAGE

Telephone Exchange (post 1941),
Anti-aircraft Operations Room
and Coastal Artillery Operations
Room

GPO telephone
equipment, and at
far end, original
Admiralty Telephone
Exchange 1939–41

ADMIRALTY CASEMATE

Naval Cipher
Office

Coding
Office

CASEMATE LEVEL TUNNELS, SUMMER 1943

Post Office
Tunnel 1941
for GPO equipment
batteries and
battery changing

Canteen
and Kitchen

Dormitories
and Offices

Napoleonic
Graffiti

Dormitories,
Offices and
Chart Store

Dormitories
and Offices

Naval Wireless
Office

Central
Communications
Office

Teleprinter Room

Emergency
Generator

Naval Cipher
Office

'Operation Dynamo'
Ops Room 1940

Admiral's
Operations Room
(from autumn 1942)

Coding and
Cipher Office

Admiral's
Staff Offices

Battery Room

Coastal Artillery
Ops Room

Anti-aircraft Ops Room
relocated from 'Z'

Admiral's
Cabin

Stores

CLIFF TERRACE

Latrines

DOVER CASTLE'S EARLY TUNNELS

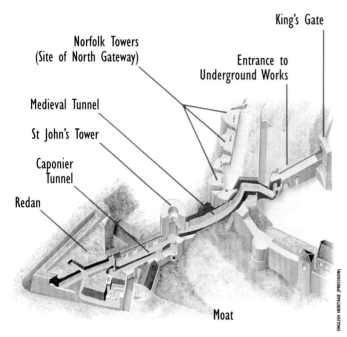

King's Gate

Norfolk Towers
(Site of North Gateway)

Entrance to
Underground Works

Medieval Tunnel

St John's Tower

Caponier
Tunnel

Redan

Moat

ENGLISH HERITAGE (PRECISION)

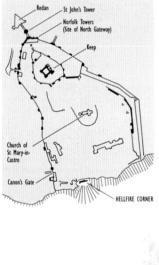

Redan · St John's Tower
Norfolk Towers
(Site of North Gateway)
Keep
Church of
St Mary-in-
Castro
Canon's Gate
HELLFIRE CORNER

ABOVE **The northern outworks of Dover Castle. Defenders had safe and speedy access here through underground tunnels**

RIGHT **In a medieval siege, an enemy could tunnel under a castle wall, causing its foundations to subside and collapse. An illustration by Ivan Lapper**

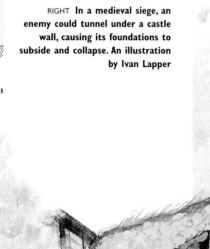

D OVER CASTLE has long been famous for its medieval tunnels. The king's engineers who constructed Henry II's great castle in the 1170s and 1180s found the chalk ideal material for cutting the defensive ditches. But it was the celebrated siege of 1216 which first alerted both attackers and defenders to the possibilities of military tunnels. That summer, Prince Louis' army surrounded the castle. Attack was concentrated on the north gateway, vulnerable from the rising ground beyond. French miners dug under the moat undermining one of the gate-towers and causing its collapse. Heroic efforts by the garrison under Hubert de Burgh to fill the breech with a timber barricade were successful and the castle was saved.

In the subsequent reconstruction and strengthening operations, the north gateway was permanently blocked and a tunnel – which can still be visited – was dug beneath it to give the garrison secure access to new defensive outworks beyond. This medieval tunnel, enlarged and extended by eighteenth and nineteenth-century military engineers, was designed for one specific purpose: to allow the garrison to reinforce vulnerable parts of the outer defences, if necessary by sallying forth and directly attacking a besieger.

ENGLISH HERITAGE (IVAN LAPPER)

— 2 —

RIGHT **Troops outside Casemate barracks in about 1840. A watercolour painting by William Burgess at Dover Museum**

BELOW **The Casemate Gallery in 1990, a view almost identical to the watercolour above**

RIGHT **Troops outside Casemate barracks in about 1840. A watercolour painting by William Burgess at Dover Museum**

NAPOLEONIC TUNNELS

It is a ditch that shall be leaped when one is daring enough to try

NAPOLEON BONAPARTE
ON THE ENGLISH CHANNEL,
16 NOVEMBER 1803

THE LATER TUNNELS behind the cliff face were built for totally different reasons. Although they made their most notable contribution during the Second World War, their origin goes back 200 years to an earlier war when Great Britain had been faced with the threat of a French invasion. Dover's nearness to France had always made it a likely target for an invading army seeking to gain a foothold in England and a secure port for its supplies. The danger was never greater than during the Revolutionary and Napoleonic Wars (1793–1815). Throughout these wars the British government poured money into fortifying the town and port. Sea-level gun batteries covered the harbour, while west of the town, massive fortifications – by far the largest built in Britain during this period – crowned Western Heights.

Dover Castle itself was strengthened. Its outer defences were reformed to much their present extent and appearance and many extra guns were mounted. As in previous wars, military planners paid especial attention to the northern and eastern defences of the castle as it was from the high ground to the north that an attack was thought most likely.

Not just the castle, but the whole of Dover became

A contemporary English cartoonist's view of Napoleon Bonaparte

an armed camp filled with thousands of troops. The soldiers were here not only to man fortifications and defend the town and harbour but also to provide a mobile force to oppose any invasion in the vicinity.

Quartering such large numbers of troops and finding storage space for supplies and munitions presented major problems. Many soldiers were accommodated in the town while hutted and tented camps on Western Heights provided further shelter. In the castle itself, the problem was acute. The existing barracks in Keep Yard were far from adequate, although these were to be supplemented by new casemates at Canon's Gate, near Bell Battery and to the rear of the Norfolk Towers.

In 1797 a radical solution was adopted. Although documentary evidence is lacking, the idea was probably the brainchild of Lieutenant Colonel William Twiss, senior engineer responsible for all military works in Dover. Faced with the need to find further space within the castle for yet more barracks, a decision was taken to excavate tunnels in from the cliff face and use these as underground accommodation for the troops.

ABOVE **Gibraltar gun casemates, excavated in the rock, overlooking Spanish territory**

At that date, no similar underground barracks existed in Britain although British military engineers had recent experience of excavating extensive tunnels for guns during the siege of Gibraltar (1779–83). At Chatham too, there was a series of tunnels giving access to gun positions in the Barrier Ditch below Fort Amherst; accommodation for the guns' crews was provided in the hillside behind the gun positions. Underground barracks at Dover had many advantages. The chalk was quick and easy to excavate and the tunnels could easily be approached down a sloping ramp from the southern side of the castle. Their entrances were too high up the cliffs to be much at risk from bombardment from French warships, while the tunnel barracks were totally impervious to any form of landward artillery barrage.

In 1797 four tunnels, or 'subterraneous bombproofs' as they were known, were driven in from the cliff face to form soldiers' accommodation. The following year a further three larger tunnels were constructed a little

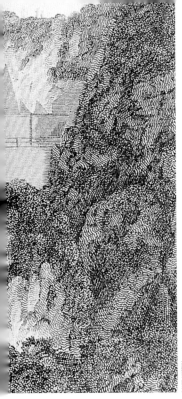

way to the east of them for the use of officers. The seven tunnels were linked near the cliff face by a winding tunnel which led to a well and to latrines located between the two groups of tunnels. A further passage or 'gallery of communication' ran to the rear of the tunnels, linking them to a second entrance within the castle.

Evidence suggests that the four tunnels for soldiers, as now, had first floors inserted which were approached by staircases midway along the two outer tunnels. There were fireplaces, while ventilation was assured by constructing vertical shafts from the head of each of the seven main accommodation tunnels to the surface of the castle above. The ends of the tunnels, overlooking the sea, had brick fronts with doors and windows for access and light.

Although the soft chalk had aided the military engineers and enabled them to complete their tunnelling by the end of 1798, it posed some problems of stability. In February 1799 there was a serious fall of chalk in the vicinity of the well while in November 1810 a large portion of the cliff face collapsed. Probably for reasons of safety as much as for health, the accommodation tunnels were largely brick-lined, although this work was not apparently completed before the end of 1810.

Pressure on accommodation was such that the first troops were moved in here certainly by the summer of 1803, construction work presumably continuing around them. No contemporary accounts have been discovered of life in these strange underground barracks during the Napoleonic Wars. Lit almost entirely by lanterns, with limited warmth provided by the few fireplaces and probably with condensation dripping from the roofs when the barracks were full, life here must have been uncomfortable if safe. We know that the troops here were provided with iron bedsteads, considered to be more hygienic than wooden ones, and an account of the castle in 1812 refers to 'several underground barracks, particularly the Royal Billy . . . where one room will contain 500 men'. If an accurate account, this would suggest that around 2000 soldiers plus officers could have lived within the cliffs.

ABOVE **Graffiti (1807), inscribed on the tunnel wall during the Napoleonic wars**

LEFT CENTRE **Royal Sappers and Miners in their working clothes in 1813**

A smugglers' cave in Langdon Cliff

WITH THE ENDING of the Napoleonic wars following the Battle of Waterloo (1815), Britain's army was rapidly reduced to its peacetime strength. The normal barracks within the castle could easily accommodate the peacetime garrison here and the cliff tunnels were emptied of troops.

The tunnels were given new uses. For long, the continuous war against smugglers had been waged largely at sea by the cutters of the Revenue Service. With the ending of the wars with France, efforts to eradicate smuggling were redoubled. In 1817 the Admiralty accepted proposals by Captain Joseph McCulloch to set up a 'coast blockade' along the Kent coast. McCulloch's scheme was to base naval seamen in the charge of lieutenants at a number of 'blockade stations' and to mount foot patrols along the beaches. Some of the bloodiest battles between smugglers and the authorities were to result. At Dover in 1818 part of the Napoleonic tunnels became the headquarters for the local blockade service.

To adapt the tunnels to the new use, the Royal Engineers cut a zig-zag ramp down to the beach and the tunnels were isolated from the castle above. Here the Coastal Blockade service remained for more than eight years. In July 1826 a skirmish with smugglers on the beach below led to the murder of Quartermaster Richard Morgan, killed by the smugglers' duck guns. Nobody claimed the very substantial reward of £500 for information leading to the murderers but from other evidence it was apparent that this was the work of the last of the Kent gangs, the Blues or the Aldington gang. Ten weeks later, Blockade officers and Bow Street Runners raided the village of Aldington at 3am and caught the gang leaders in their beds. With the break-up of this gang, large scale smuggling in Kent was virtually at an end.

Already by 1826 the Coast Blockade was finding the cliff casemates inconveniently far from the beaches and in late 1827 or early 1828 it obtained permission to relocate in the Congreve Rocket Shed beside Guildford Battery below the castle. The rockets were removed to the cliff casemates and stored alongside the gunpowder barrels which already occupied most of the space which had not been used by the Coast Blockade. For some years the tunnels remained a huge ammunition store before being emptied. Later in the nineteenth century, most probably in the 1870s, a spiral staircase was cut to link the rear passage of the tunnels with a new exit a little to the south-west of the Victorian Officers' Mess. By the end of the nineteenth century however the tunnels appear to have been abandoned.

RIGGING of a SMUGGLER.

In this Rowlandson print a woman smuggler is shown being 'rigged out' with brandy, perfume, cigars, teas and other contraband, which she hides beneath her voluminous dress

BELOW **Officers of the Coast Blockade fighting smugglers**

FIRST WORLD WAR

Warships in the Admiralty Harbour, Dover, early this century. The dockyard in the foreground is now the site of the eastern ferry terminals

I N 1905 THE ARMY established a Fire Command Post on the cliff edge above the tunnels; this controlled and directed the fire of the seaward gun batteries. On the outbreak of war in 1914 the Admiralty transferred its Port War Signal Station and a wireless telegraphy apparatus here from Western Heights.

By 1914, Dover had become an important naval station, the new 610-acre Admiralty Harbour giving the only safe haven for warships between the Nore and Portsmouth. Throughout the First World War Dover was a key naval station, providing escorts for the troop and supply convoys to France and mounting patrols in the Dover Straits to counter enemy submarines and surface warships. By 1917, over 400 vessels formed the Dover Patrol. If the tunnels had a use then, it was probably only for storage.

AFTER THE MUNICH CRISIS of 1938, when it became apparent that war with Germany was becoming inevitable, an urgent reassessment was undertaken of the country's defences. At Dover, one of the prime needs was for a secure headquarters, impervious to bombing. The old Napoleonic tunnels were ideal, and 1938 plans envisaged their use by the navy, by the fortress commander and as coastal and anti-aircraft operations centres.

In August 1939, the outbreak of war with Germany imminent, Vice-Admiral Bertram Ramsay was appointed Vice-Admiral Dover, charged with denying the Straits to enemy naval forces and securing the safety of allied cross-Channel shipping. Ramsay had served in the famous Dover Patrol from 1915 to 1918, latterly in command of HMS *Broke*, and he knew the area well. He and his naval staff moved in beneath the castle, principally occupying the easternmost casemate.

Anti-aircraft gun at Dover in 1941/42. Note the terrace of the Casemate tunnels in the cliff face behind

LEFT **Reconstructed telephone and telex exchange, part of the communications centre in the tunnels. The exchange was located here in 1941**

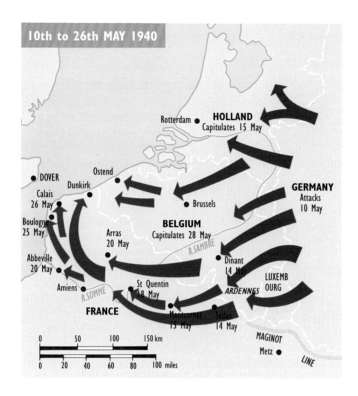

Rotterdam
HOLLAND
Capitulates 15 May

DOVER
Ostend
Dunkirk
Calais
26 May
Boulogne
25 May
Arras
20 May
BELGIUM
Capitulates 28 May
Brussels
GERMANY
Attacks
10 May

Abbeville
20 May
R.SAMBRE
Dinant
14 May
LUXEMB
OURG
Amiens
R.SOMME
St Quentin
18 May
ARDENNES
FRANCE
Montcornet
15 May
Sedan
14 May
MAGINOT
Metz
LINE

0   50   100   150 km
0   20   40   60   80   100 miles

LEFT **The German attack in May 1940 was rapid. Within two weeks, Panzer divisions, deploying 1800 tanks, had broken through to the French coast, effectively cutting off the British and some French troops from the main French army**

RIGHT **German Panzer divisions sweeping through the Belgian and French countryside. This rapidly moving attack became known as a** *Blitzkrieg*

Vice-Admiral Ramsay, who masterminded the evacuation of the trapped English and French armies from Dunkirk in May and June 1940

OPERATION DYNAMO: PREPARATIONS

O N 10 MAY 1940 Hitler's armies struck westwards across Europe. Within three weeks Holland and Belgium had surrendered and German Panzer divisions (tank forces) had split the British and French armies. The British Expeditionary Force (BEF) and a substantial number of French troops were trapped in a diminishing pocket of land centred on the port of Dunkirk. On 25 May Boulogne was captured; the following day Calais fell. That evening the British government ordered the evacuation of as many men as possible of the BEF. Vice-Admiral Ramsay, in charge of the operation, had been given less than a week to prepare.

During the Second World War, the Admiralty Casemate as it became known, was partitioned into a number of offices. The largest was Ramsay's Operations Room. In here he directed and inspired a small staff who had the awesome task of planning the evacuation of up to 400,000 British and French troops under constant attack from German forces. The evacuation plan was codenamed *Operation Dynamo*.

By 26 May Ramsay had assembled 15 passenger ferries at Dover and a further 20 at Southampton. These, it was hoped, would be able to embark troops direct

ULLSTEIN BILDERDIENST

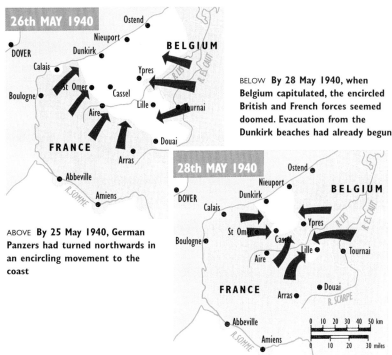

26th MAY 1940

BELOW **By 28 May 1940, when Belgium capitulated, the encircled British and French forces seemed doomed. Evacuation from the Dunkirk beaches had already begun**

ABOVE **By 25 May 1940, German Panzers had turned northwards in an encircling movement to the coast**

28th MAY 1940

from the quays at Dunkirk. To help in the evacuation and to provide escorts for the merchant ships Ramsay had a force of destroyers, corvettes, minesweepers and naval trawlers. These ships were augmented by cargo vessels, coasters and some 40 Dutch self-propelled barges, known to the navy who manned them as 'skoots'. All ships of the British merchant marine had their normal civilian crews, both men and women. But as sheer exhaustion and the near-continuous bombing and shelling began to take their toll, naval personnel were drafted in to help where needed.

Behind this effort lay frantic round-the-clock work in the cliff tunnels. A naval staff-officer called it 'organised chaos'. Telephone calls to the Nore Command for further destroyers, telephone calls to the Ministry of Shipping for merchant ships, liaison with the Southern Railway for special troop trains, calls to the Admiralty for tugs, weapons, ammunition, medical supplies, spare parts, fuel, rations and above all, trained personnel. The phone calls were endless. On 23 May Ramsay wrote to his wife 'no bed for any of us last night, and probably not for many nights'. Two days later, he wrote again 'days and nights are all one'. A little later 'All my staff are completely worn out, yet I see no prospect of any let up'. On 27 May, some relief was provided by the arrival of Vice-Admiral Sir James Somerville. As the military situation worsened, naval plans repeatedly had to be changed, revised or abandoned. Instant decisions had to be made, frequently from confused and conflicting messages.

LEFT **'Operation Dynamo' control room in the Admiralty Casemate at Dover**

DOVER MUSEUM

BELOW **Vice-Admiral Ramsay's 'Cabin' at the end of the Admiralty Casemate. The window looked out on to Dover harbour and the Channel**

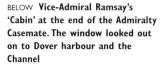

IMPERIAL WAR MUSEUM

OPERATION DYNAMO: DUNKIRK EVACUATION
26 MAY TO 3 JUNE 1940

ABOVE **Dunkirk harbour, oil tanks ablaze from German bombing. In the foreground are the two moles**

RIGHT **Map of Dunkirk harbour and beaches**

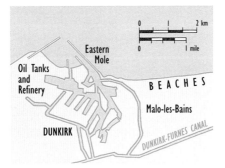

BELOW **Troops wading out from the beaches to board ships. The slowness of this method is apparent**

AT 1857 HOURS on 26 May 1940 Ramsay received a formal signal to commence Operation Dynamo. At best, the Admiralty hoped that 45,000 troops might be saved in the two days before Dunkirk was expected to fall.

Minefields and shelling from German batteries on the French coast forced the evacuation convoys to take longer routes to Dunkirk. The first convoy, after sustaining heavy air attacks, found Dunkirk port and its oil tanks ablaze from bombing. Only the passenger ferries *Royal Daffodil* and later the *Canterbury* succeeded in berthing. By the end of the first day only seven and a half thousand troops had been rescued and it was clearly impossible to use the port.

At Dunkirk, Captain Tennant in charge of the naval shore party, signalled for rescue ships to be diverted to the beaches east of the town. But here, shallow waters meant that even at high tide a destroyer could not approach within a mile of the shore. Troops had to be ferried out in ships' lifeboats and small craft. Rescue was painfully slow and there was a desperate need for small boats. But there was a possible alternative. Running out nearly 1300m (4250ft) from the eastern side of the harbour was the eastern mole, a spindly concrete-legged structure with a narrow timber walkway. It was not designed to withstand ships berthing against it, but in this dire emergency it was worth trying.

At 2230 hours on the night of 27 May, Tennant ordered the *Queen of the Channel* alongside. 950 men scrambled aboard, and though the ship was to be sunk on her way back to Dover, she had proved that the mole was usable. From then on, small ships operated off the beaches, but large vessels queued for the mole. Differences in loading speeds were dramatic: HMS *Sabre* took two hours to load 100 men from the beach, but alongside the mole 500 troops boarded in 35 minutes.

Beneath Dover Castle Ramsay was still asking for all available Royal Navy destroyers. More were sent from Portsmouth, others from the Nore Command. HMS *Jaguar* sped down from convoy duties off Norway, others came from the Western Approaches. Dover harbour was crowded with vessels unloading, taking on fresh supplies and heading back across the Straits. Wounded were helped ashore, many were tended by medical staff on the quayside; troops in many cases were given their first food for days before being put on

German MEII0 aircraft flying over the ruined town of Dunkirk

ULLSTEIN BILDERDIENST

BELOW **Boarding troops from the eastern mole at Dunkirk. Despite the dangers, embarkation proved much speedier than from the beaches**

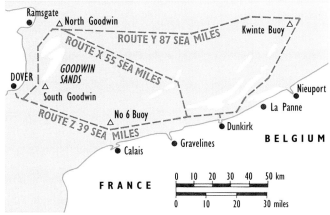

ROUTE Y 87 SEA MILES

ROUTE X 55 SEA MILES

ROUTE Z 39 SEA MILES

Ramsgate
North Goodwin
Kwinte Buoy
DOVER
GOODWIN SANDS
South Goodwin
Nieuport
No 6 Buoy
La Panne
Dunkirk
BELGIUM
Gravelines
Calais
FRANCE

0 10 20 30 40 50 km
0 10 20 30 miles

ABOVE **The three evacuation routes between Dunkirk and Dover**

BELOW **The Channel ferry *Canterbury*. Built in 1929 to carry only 300 first class passengers, she succeeded in accommodating 2000 troops at Dunkirk on 29 May 1940**

NATIONAL MARITIME MUSEUM

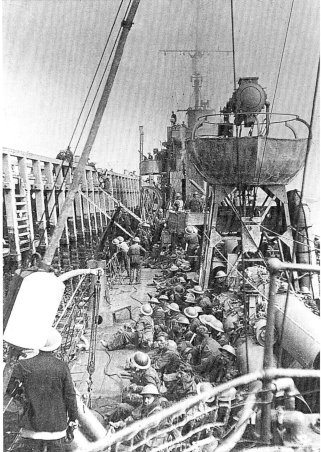

Isle of Man steamship *Mona's Queen* breaking in two, after striking a mine half-a-mile from Dunkirk on 29 May 1940

Naval vessels crowding the quays at Dover. At the height of the Dunkirk evacuation, vessels lay alongside three or four deep

BELOW   Troop train preparing to leave Dover. The Southern Railway provided 327 special trains during the Dunkirk evacuation

special trains. In all, the Southern Railway provided some 327 troop trains from Dover during the nine days of the evacuation. The story was repeated at Margate, Ramsgate and Folkestone.

In London, the Admiralty's Small Vessels Pool was busy collecting all readily-available seaworthy pleasure craft. They came from the Thames, the Medway, east coast ports, the harbours and creeks of southern England. Volunteer crews, many of whom had never sailed out of sight of land before, were sent in flotillas to Sheerness Dockyard. Here, the navy checked the boats, issued fuel, rations and charts and organised them in convoys to wait at Ramsgate for final sailing orders.

These pleasure craft were joined by a multitude of other ships: fishing smacks, lifeboats, trawlers, drifters, the Hayling Island ferries, Thames sailing barges, the Leigh-on-Sea cockle boats, lifeboats from liners in port. Tugs were sent by the great towage companies – London Docks had only one tug left; Newhaven, Portsmouth and Southampton were similarly divested.

From Ramsgate, the first convoy of 'little ships' sailed at 2200 hours in the evening of 29 May. By next day they were streaming across the Channel in seemingly unending lines. On the bridge of the destroyer HMS *Malcolm*, heading back laden with troops from Dunkirk, the sight of the 'little ships' reminded the First Lieutenant of the St Crispin's Day speech in Shakespeare's *Henry V*:

> And Gentlemen of England, now abed
> Shall think themselves accurs'd they were not here.

Fortunately, throughout the evacuation, the seas remained abnormally calm. Most of the small craft headed for the beaches to act as tenders; some of the larger trawlers and drifters loaded troops directly in Dunkirk harbour.

By then, nobody had any illusions as to the dangers. At first a huge pall of smoke hid Dunkirk harbour and gave a measure of protection, but when a breeze blew it clear on the afternoon of 29 May, over 400 German aircraft attacked. In the crowded conditions at the end of the mole, the bombers could hardly miss. The destroyer *Jaguar* was damaged, HMS *Grenade* was hit and later blew up. The paddle-minesweeper *Waverley* was bombed on the way home with the loss of over 400 troops. The passenger ships *Lorina* and *Normannia* were bombed and sunk. Despite their best efforts, the Royal Air Force could give only limited protection.

Ships faced other hazards. The French destroyer *Bourrasque* with 800 on board hit a mine on 30 May. The previous night, the destroyer HMS *Wakeful* laden with over 600 troops was torpedoed off the Kwinte Buoy and sank in 15 seconds. HMS *Grafton*, with 800 troops on board, was torpedoed as she stopped to rescue the few survivors. In the wake of this tragedy, Ramsay had to signal 'Vessels carrying troops, not to stop to pick up

RIGHT **French destroyer *Bourrasque* sinking after striking a mine on 30 May 1940. As she went down, her own depth charges exploded, killing many men as they struggled in the water**

survivors from ships sunk but are to inform other nearby ships'.

Sunken ships made navigation hazardous. The elderly minesweeper *Brighton Belle* sank after colliding with a hidden wreck; her 800 troops were rescued by the *Medway Queen*. By 29 May so many destroyers had been sunk or damaged that the Admiralty reluctantly withdrew the eight newest and largest – they would be vital in future battles. But the destroyers and passenger ships were even more crucial in this battle for only they had the carrying capacity to lift the numbers of troops. In desperation on 30 May Ramsay telephoned the First Sea Lord and six of the eight were returned to him.

ABOVE **HMS *Vivacious* alongside the Dunkirk mole, just after an air attack that sank the trawler in the foreground**

LEFT **Laden with troops, a British drifter heads for England from blazing Dunkirk. The drifter is either the *Lord Cavan* or the *Jacketa***

In Dunkirk, troops waited sheltering in cellars and houses; on the beaches they sought protection in the sand dunes. Makeshift jetties were constructed using army lorries. Everywhere, troops queued, long lines snaking into the water. On 30 May, heavy cloud prevented air attacks, but 1 June was fine and clear. In the first hours of daylight, the warships *Havant*, *Keith* and *Skipjack* were sunk. By that evening a total of 31 ships had been destroyed and eleven seriously damaged. Abandoned and blazing vessels could be seen all along the beaches. It was clear that from now on, relief ships would have to operate only at night. That evening Ramsay dispatched eight destroyers and seven passenger ships to the east mole; a multitude of smaller vessels headed for the beaches. Navigation lights were not permitted, adding to the hazards. Despite the disasters of the day, nearly 65,000 troops were picked up, bringing the tally of those saved to 287,000.

The following day in broad daylight, Ramsay attempted to rescue the badly wounded troops. The hospital ships, the ferries *Worthing* and *Paris*, clearly marked with red crosses like their sister ship, the *Dinard*, sailed unescorted from Dover. Subjected to ferocious air attacks and sustaining considerable damage, they were forced to abandon their mission.

That evening, Ramsay despatched an even larger force, at its centre 13 passenger ships, 14 minesweepers and 11 destroyers. At 2330 hours that night Captain Tennant sent the historic signal from Dunkirk 'BEF evacuated'.

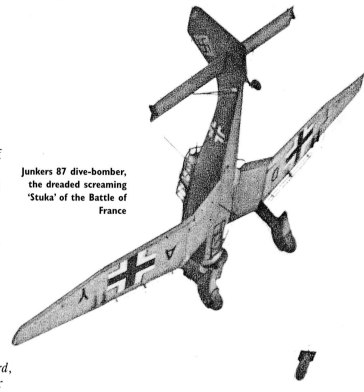

Junkers 87 dive-bomber, the dreaded screaming 'Stuka' of the Battle of France

BELOW **British troops on the Dunkirk beach during an air-attack. Note the explosions at sea and in the air** ROBERT HUNT LIBRARY

IMPERIAL WAR MUSEUM

IMPERIAL WAR MUSEUM

ULLSTEIN BILDERDIENST

IMPERIAL WAR MUSEUM

LEFT **Makeshift jetty built of army lorries**

ABOVE **Charles Cundall's evocative painting of the Dunkirk evacuation**

BELOW LEFT **HMS *Havant* arriving in Dover harbour, laden with troops from Dunkirk**

BELOW **Perimeter line held by the French and British at Dunkirk on 31 May 1940**

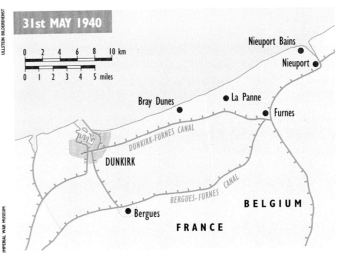

31st MAY 1940

0 2 4 6 8 10 km
0 1 2 3 4 5 miles

Nieuport Bains
Nieuport
Bray Dunes
La Panne
Furnes
DUNKIRK-FURNES CANAL
DUNKIRK
BERGUES-FURNES CANAL
BELGIUM
Bergues
FRANCE

By now, the German forces were nearly in the outskirts of the town. Only one more night evacuation was possible. On the night of 3 June a final effort was made using British, French, Belgian and Dutch ships to bring out as many of the French rearguard as possible. Over 26,000 were saved.

The last Royal Navy ship to enter Dunkirk harbour was a small Motor Torpedo Boat. Her captain recorded 'The night was very dark and full of rushing shapes, all of which appeared to be coming directly at us. They were the last of the rescue ships completing their final task. The flames over the city did not seem so fierce as the night before, but the pall of smoke, which none who saw it will ever forget, still streamed westward from the dying town, and the ring of gun flashes had closed in in an ever narrowing circle . . . The whole scene was filled with a sense of finality and death; the curtain was ringing down on a great tragedy'.

A week before, it might have been total tragedy, with most of the British army lost. But on the afternoon of 4 June, the Prime Minister Winston Churchill was able to say to a packed House of Commons 'When a week ago I asked the House to fix this afternoon for a statement, I feared it would be my hard lot to announce from this box the greatest military disaster in our long history'. Instead, he was able to tell them of the 'miracle' of Dunkirk, the extraordinary evacuation, in which over 338,000 troops were brought back – the whole of the BEF at Dunkirk and 139,000 French soldiers. But Churchill warned his listeners, 'We must be very careful not to assign to this deliverance the attributes of a victory. Wars are not won by evacuations'.

The price had been high. The army had lost virtually all its heavy equipment. 693 British ships had taken part. 188 of the smaller craft had been sunk as well as eight passenger ships, a hospital ship, trawlers, minesweepers, a sloop and six destroyers. Many others had been seriously damaged – out of more than forty destroyers which had taken part, only 13 remained fit for immediate service. But had it not been for the organising genius, the leadership and drive of Vice-Admiral Ramsay in his command centre underneath Dover Castle, the evacuation might never have achieved its extraordinary results. Certainly an author and journalist who himself manned one of the 'little ships' had no doubts, later writing:

> 'It is given to few men to command a miracle. It was so given to Bertram Home Ramsay, and the frail iron balcony that juts from the embrasure of the old casemate in the Dover cliff was the quarter deck from which he commanded one of the great campaigns in the sea story of Britain.'

LEFT **A wounded soldier is given a drink on the quay at Dover**

LEFT **British troops, exhausted from their ordeal, disembarking at Dover**

ABOVE **Vice-Admiral Ramsay on the cliff balcony at the end of the Admiralty Casemate**

LEFT **Norman Wilkinson's painting 'The Little Ships at Dunkirk in June 1940'**

ABOVE **Muirhead Bone's pencil sketch of troops arriving at Dover in vessels both large and small**

BELOW **The aftermath at Dunkirk: dead soldiers and abandoned vehicles**

DUNKIRK EVACUATION – DAILY FIGURES	
26th May	4,247
27th May	5,718
28th May	18,527
29th May	50,331
30th May	53,227
31st May	64,141
1st June	61,557
2nd June	23,604
3rd June	29,641
4th June	27,689
TOTAL	**338,682**

BELOW **A wounded French soldier being taken ashore by stretcher**

DOVER CASTLE: FRONT-LINE FORTRESS

BELOW **One of a battery of 14-inch guns at Dover**

BELOW **On I July 1940, nine days after the French armistice, Herman Goering (sixth from right) and his senior staff gaze across the Straits of Dover to England**

WITH THE FALL OF FRANCE in June 1940, Dover found itself in the front line. A German invasion was daily expected and amongst the many frantic preparations to counter this, the castle was provisioned to withstand a six-week siege. For the next four years town and harbour were to be the targets for German bombs and shells. In this situation, the secure tunnels beneath the castle assumed even greater importance. What in 1939 had been a mainly naval headquarters with liaison officers from the army and air force, ultimately blossomed in 1943 into a Combined Headquarters for all three services.

All those who worked down here, both service and civilian, recall the long hours, the uneven chalk floors in the communication tunnels, and the strain and weariness

ABOVE **Civilians sheltering in the town caves at Dover**

of the underground existence. The atmosphere frequently was chill and damp while the lack of daylight and the constant background roar of the later forced ventilation added to feelings of tiredness. Except in emergencies, or when air raids or shelling prevented them from leaving, personnel in the early years of the war never slept in the tunnels.

Conditions in the tunnels and the comparative lack of facilities for personnel were worse before the completion of extra accommodation in 1941/42. There was however little time for considerations of personal discomfort. Within three weeks of the Dunkirk evacuation, France had surrendered. Out in the Channel, British convoys were subjected to ferocious air attacks, the preliminary to the Battle of Britain, fought overhead from mid-July to mid-September 1940. Although the defeat of the *Luftwaffe* signalled the end of any invasion for the rest of 1940, the threat remained a real one until 1942.

ABOVE **Prime Minister Winston Churchill (right) watches an air battle from the Casemate gallery on 28 August 1940**

IMPERIAL WAR MUSEUM

ABOVE **The suicidal attack of naval Swordfish torpedo-bombers on the German battle-cruisers** *Scharnhorst* **and** *Gneisenau* **on 12 February 1942. A painting by Norman Wilkinson**

BELOW **Map of the German battle-cruisers' dash through the English Channel**

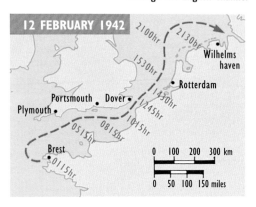

Throughout the war, there was constant skirmishing between German E-boats and Royal Navy Motor Torpedo Boats and Motor Gun Boats. Long-range guns on both shores fired across the Straits, usually at convoys or single merchantmen attempting the dangerous passage. Occasionally there were greater excitements as on 12 February 1942 when the powerful German battle-cruisers *Scharnhorst* and *Gneisenau* together with the cruiser *Prinz Eugen* staged their daring dash through the Straits flanked by flotillas of destroyers and torpedo boats and with an umbrella of fighters above.

Within the tunnels, all this activity was monitored and appropriate action ordered. Information flowed in from coastal observers, pilots and warships, from intelligence gathering elsewhere, and from the new radar chain whose lattice masts were a prominent feature on the cliff top east of the castle. In the early months of the war, the tunnels were mainly a naval

ABOVE **German shells bursting among the radar masts at Dover.**

headquarters, but, as coastal artillery and anti-aircraft batteries expanded, their operations rooms were established in the tunnels adjacent to the Admiralty Casemate. Gun batteries from the North Foreland as far west as Hastings were controlled from here. By January 1941 the strength of coastal artillery in this sector numbered nearly four-and-a-half thousand troops.

Coastal artillery and naval ships were all deployed from the tunnel headquarters, which was also in close communication with the RAF. From early on, the navy also employed fluent German speakers next to the cipher room in the Admiralty casemate. These listened to wireless transmissions on the German forces radio frequencies and on occasion attempted to confuse the enemy by broadcasting misleading orders.

ABOVE **WRNS switchboard operator on duty in the casemate tunnels**

RIGHT **Coastal artillery plotting room in the tunnel headquarters. This room controlled batteries from Hastings to the North Foreland**

CREATION OF COMBINED HEADQUARTERS' TUNNELS
1941–43

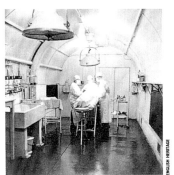 

LEFT **Hospital operating theatre and kitchens at Annexe level**

MEANWHILE, with growing pressure for space in the existing tunnels, a decision was taken early in 1941 to extend the system. Three army tunnelling companies were brought in and excavations began in three different places. An upper level of tunnels, forming a grid pattern, was begun a little to the west of the existing Napoleonic level which was known as 'Casemate Level'. The new tunnels, named 'Annexe', initially were used as a hospital and dressing station, but later became dormitories.

On the Casemate level itself, the proliferation of communication equipment led to the digging of a tunnel west of and parallel to the three eastern tunnels. This was for the use of the General Post Office, who had charge of all the land communications and needed the space for the dozens of batteries and battery-charging equipment needed by the telephone and teleprinter systems. In the chalk between the Admiralty Casemate and the tunnel housing the coastal artillery, anti-aircraft operations rooms and the main telephone exchange, a tunnel was excavated from the rear communication tunnel. This gave direct access to the operations rooms, bypassing the telephone exchange.

Graffiti on the Casemate walls, covering the period 1860 to 1942

The major construction work in 1941 was concentrated on excavating a vast new Combined Headquarters complex to the rear of 'Casemate Level'. This was part of the long-term preparations for the invasion of France and paralleled similar protected headquarters constructed at Devonport and Portsmouth. When Normandy was selected as the invasion point, the Portsmouth CHQ played the key role. None of the primary planning for the 1944 Normandy landings was done at Dover, but this headquarters was needed to handle much of the operational work undertaken by the three services in this area.

LEFT **A reconstruction of the Anti-Aircraft Operations Room. The course of enemy aircraft were charted on the illuminated screens and co-ordinated on the plotting tables**

The new tunnel system was to have a central Operations Room for all three services surrounded by offices and other facilities. To avoid disturbing the Admiralty headquarters, a works tunnel was driven in from the east moat of the castle and spoil was removed through it. However, work was also begun on a tunnel within Casemates level running parallel with the rear communication tunnel from the base of the spiral stairs. This was to link through with the new headquarters complex – codenamed *Bastion* – when the latter was completed. However, when some fifty percent of the excavations had been finished, serious rock falls and subsidences led to the abandonment of this project and these tunnels have remained sealed ever since.

Faced with this major set-back, a decision was taken in 1942 to excavate a further grid of tunnels some fifty feet below the Napoleonic tunnels. This new level, codenamed *Dumpy*, was completed and the Combined Headquarters was brought into operation down here in the summer of 1943. However, the navy and coastal artillery, already well-established at Casemate level and with a more narrowly focused role defending the Straits, chose to retain their existing accommodation above. Similarly, much of the communication equipment remained in the adjacent tunnels.

For the rest of the war, Dover continued to play a vital role. There were ambitious plans to excavate yet further levels of tunnels but the war ended before much had been done.

Dormitories at the Annexe level. A sketch by the war artist, Anthony Gross

RIGHT **The reconstructed Repeater Station, part of the communications network**

AFTER THE WAR only the Admiralty retained an interest here. In 1958 the navy abandoned the tunnels which were handed over to the Home Office to be adapted to form one of ten proposed Regional Seats of Government in England. This was the time of the Cold War, fear of Russian intentions, and the 'three-minute warning' of nuclear attack. The Cuban Missile Crisis of 1962 was to bring the world to the brink of nuclear war. Regional Seats of Government, located in relatively secure accommodation, were intended to function during and after a nuclear attack which, it was assumed, would have destroyed London and the main government machinery.

Under the threat of a major war, it was planned that senior ministers would be appointed as Regional Commissioners to take charge of areas of the country. Amidst the devastation and carnage of a post-nuclear Britain, their task would be to ensure a degree of law and order, to make the best use of remaining resources and to maintain some of the machinery of administration. Aided by a small team of civilian and military advisers, they would have virtually unfettered powers over the surviving population. It was assumed that each region would need to act virtually independently of the others.

The Dover tunnels had been planned for conventional warfare. To fit them for their new role, the Home Office spent large sums of money modernising the lowest tier of tunnels forming the old Combined Headquarters. New communications equipment, modern air-filtration plant and improved generators were installed. Space was found for large reserves of fuel and water; the old spiral stairs to the surface had a concrete capping added as part of precautions against nuclear contamination. A new lift was added. On the Casemate level, the three eastern tunnels, once Ramsay's headquarters, the local command centres for the coastal artillery, the anti-aircraft operations room and the old telephone exchange, were abandoned and their contents finally removed. The western group of tunnels however were modernised to become dormitories and mess rooms. These, little altered, form the present visitor centre at the tunnels.

In 1984 the Home Office finally abandoned the Dover tunnels after removing virtually all the equipment. Nowhere else is it possible to see such a remarkable underground complex, originally conceived as secure barracks, finding its greatest role during nine days in 1940, and mercifully never being put to the test during its final phase.

Atomic bomb cloud over Nagasaki in August 1945, signalling the end of the war in Asia, but heralding the nuclear cold war